The Walking With God Series

Friendship With God
Developing Intimacy With God

Don Cousins & Judson Poling

Zondervan Publishing House
Grand Rapids, Michigan

A Division of HarperCollinsPublishers

WILLOW CREEK RESOURCES

The Walking With God Series

Friendship With God:
Developing Intimacy with God

The Incomparable Jesus:
Experiencing the Power of Christ

"Follow Me!":
Walking with Jesus in Everyday Life

Discovering the Church:
Becoming Part of God's New Community

Building Your Church:
Using Your Gifts, Time, and Resources

Impacting Your World:
Becoming a Person of Influence

Published by Zondervan Publishing House, Grand Rapids, Michigan 49530. Produced by The Livingstone Corporation. James C. Galvin, J. Michael Kendrick, and Daryl J. Lucas, and Darcy J. Kamps, project staff.

ISBN 0-310-59143-0

Cover design: Mark Veldheer
Interior design: Catherine Bergstrom

Printed in the United States of America
96 97 98 99 / DP / 9 8

Preface

The *Walking With God Series* was developed as the curriculum for small groups at Willow Creek Community Church in South Barrington, Illinois. This innovative church has grown to over 15,000 in less than two decades, and the material here flows out of the vision and values of this dynamic ministry. Groups using these studies have produced many of the leaders, both staff and volunteer, throughout the church.

Associate Pastor Don Cousins wrote the first draft of this material and used it with his own small group. After testing it there, he revised it and passed his notes to Judson Poling, Director of Curriculum Development, who edited and expanded the outlines. Several pilot groups helped shape the material as it was being written and revised. A team of leaders labored through a line-by-line revision of these study guides over a year's span of time. Finally, these revisions were put into this new, more usable format.

Any church or group can use these studies in a relational context to help raise up devoted disciples. Group members who finish all six books will lay a solid foundation for a lifelong walk with God.

Willow Creek Resources is a publishing partnership between Zondervan Publishing House and the Willow Creek Association. Willow Creek Resources will include drama sketches, small group curricula, training material, videos, and many other specialized ministry resources.

Willow Creek Association is an international network of churches ministering to the unchurched. Founded in 1992, the Willow Creek Association serves churches through conferences, seminars, regional roundtables, consulting, and ministry resource materials. The mission of the Association is to assist churches in reestablishing the priority and practice of reaching lost people for Christ through church ministries targeted to seekers.

For conference and seminar information please write to:

Willow Creek Association
P.O. Box 3188
Barrington, Illinois 60011-3188

Contents

Friendship With God

Developing Intimacy With God

Introduction 11

1. A Friend Worth Having 13

2. How to be Sure You're a Christian 19

3. God's Word to You 29

4. God's Word in You 35

5. Taking God's Word to Heart 41

6. Ground Rules for Prayer 45

7. Let's Pray 49

8. Getting Together With God 53

9. The Role of the Holy Spirit 59

10. Being Filled With the Spirit 63

11. How to be Filled With the Spirit 67

12. Grieving the Holy Spirit 73

13. Reviewing *Friendship With God* 77

Friendship With God

Developing Intimacy with God

Introduction

At its core, Christianity is Christ. Christians embrace a Person, not merely a philosophy. It is not knowing about his teaching so much as it is knowing him. The greatest misunderstanding about Christianity today, even in the church, is the perception that God's bottom-line requirements are deeds to be done and beliefs to be believed. The Christ who spoke is bypassed for the things he spoke; the Guide is left behind for the guidance; the Commander is ignored in the carrying out of commands. The *Walking With God Series* addresses this problem by encouraging the Christian to develop a relationship with the living God.

This series is based on the belief that a disciple is one who

- walks with God

- lives the Word

- contributes to the work

- impacts the world

So we begin this curriculum with a study of that essential relationship (*Friendship With God*). The next two study guides are an examination of the life of Jesus (*The Incomparable Jesus* and *"Follow Me!"*). After that, we learn of our place in the gathering of believers known as the church (*Discovering the Church* and *Building Your Church*). Finally, we conclude by learning ways to make our mark for his kingdom (*Impacting Your World*).

We do not intend to bury people in mountains of theological information. Our interest lies in transforming hearts. We'd readily recommend two years of a small group experience that truly caused people to know God over twenty years of "Christian education" that rendered them all but dead to the real world and the God who is willing to walk with them in it. Bible studies alone won't produce that change. Thus, we have designed the assignments as a subtle way of getting people to begin their own times alone with God. Ultimately, the success of this study will depend on how consistently you walk with God after the study is over.

A Friend Worth Having

Suppose you have to choose between two people who want to go to dinner with you. The first person is very warm and takes a genuine interest in others. He listens attentively and is fun to be with. Those who develop a friendship with him want it to last a lifetime.

In contrast, the second person is aloof and demanding. He keeps most of his friends (if you could call them that) at a distance. The only time he calls is when he wants something from you. He's pretty unpredictable emotionally, and you never quite know where you stand with him. He wields considerable influence, but if it weren't for his power he probably wouldn't have any friends at all. If you're like most people, you'd rather have dinner with the first person.

Who is God like in your mind—the first person or the second? Unfortunately, many people have a distorted view of God's character. To them, he's much like the second person—distant and uncaring. Although he is powerful, he can't be counted on. The only real benefit in knowing him comes from occasional answers to prayer. No wonder people have a hard time relating to him! Who would want to cultivate a friendship like that?

If your view of God has been been colored by mistaken assumptions and erroneous ideas, it can be startling to learn that God longs to establish a close, intimate friendship with you. This study will help you understand what it means to relate to God in a personal way. Let this one truth sink in: *God is a Friend worth having.*

What are some necessary ingredients for building a relationship with another person?

What are some necessary ingredients for a relationship with God?

Why We Can Have a Personal Relationship with God

1 God has chosen us.

Why is it significant that Jesus said, "I chose you?" (John 15:16)

2 God wants to spend time with us.

What does it mean when Jesus says that he wants to eat with you? (Revelation 3:20)

3 God will never leave us.

How do you respond to the promise that God will never leave us? (Hebrews 13:5)

What God Has Given Us to Establish This Relationship

1   He gave us his Son.

What did God accomplish for us through giving his Son? (John 3:16)

2   He gave us a book.

Why is the Bible so important for our relationship with God? (Matthew 4:4)

3   He gave us his Spirit.

What does the Holy Spirit do for us? (John 16:13-14)

Now that you see how much God has done to establish a relationship with you, what is your response?

Bible

Schedule three times this week to get alone with God. Pick the time during the day that works best for you. Each time, read one of the first three chapters from the Gospel of John and write down one idea for application. Make a list of what you learn about Jesus from your study. Also, read over the "Benefits of a Relationship with God" in your study guide.

Prayer

Spend a few minutes praying about things that come to mind during your Bible reading. At the end of the week list two or three benefits you received from these appointments with God.

Scripture Memory

As part of the curriculum, we've included memory verses with each study. If you desire to make this discipline part of your discipleship experience, begin by memorizing this verse:

Here I am! I stand at the door and knock. If anyone hears my voice and opens the door, I will come in and eat with him, and he with me.   Revelation 3:20

Next week we will explore the topic of how to be sure you are a Christian. If you want to prepare for the discussion, think about a time you made a major decision in life (new job, major purchase, move to another city). What factors made you feel certain about your decision? You could also compare two relationships in your life—one where you knew where you stood with the person and one where you didn't. How did this knowledge affect the relationships?

Benefits of a Relationship with God

Relationships

Marriage, friendships, interaction with fellow-workers can all be renewed when you are in a right relationship with God . . . new love, new concern, new depth—not to mention all the new and different people you'll meet by participating in a local church.

Peace

The restlessness produced by unforgiven sin and purposeless activities ceases. St. Augustine in the fourth century said, "You have made us for Yourself, O God, and our hearts are restless until they find their rest in You."

Purpose

At best, life without Christ gives way to an agenda or cause; at worst, it degenerates into total self-seeking. With Christ, our lives come under the direction and guidance of an all-loving Spirit who has our best interests continuously in mind and leads us along the path of greatest significance. Any and every action we do in the Spirit has eternal value.

Fulfillment

Not just purpose and significance in life, but great satisfaction becomes the birthright of every believer. Even hard times do not diminish the sense of joy as we grow into who he created us to be.

Direction

The limited, finite perspectives on life are replaced by the counsel of an infinitely wise Advisor. All decisions, big or small, become his concerns as well as ours. Although common sense enables a Christian to choose the right path in most circumstances, God invests himself for our good and his glory in the outcome of *every* choice.

Confidence

In 1 John 4:18, the Bible says, "Perfect love drives out fear." This includes: fear of punishment (Christ already took that); fear of failure ("If God is for us, who can be against us?" [Romans 8:31]); fear of intimidation (any of our enemies are no match for the Lord); fear of loss (all that we have now belongs to Christ—his glory in us will never be hindered by any material or circumstantial fluctuations); fear of rejection (even if all others abandon us, he will never leave us nor forsake us [see Hebrews 13:5]).

Self-Esteem

We usually do not see ourselves for who we really are; we view ourselves as what we think *others* think we are. If parents and others have constantly found fault with us, we will find fault with ourselves. No matter how objective we try to be about it, our self-esteem is to some extent at the mercy of those whom we consider important to us. When God becomes important to us, his view of us will supersede all others—and his Word abounds with promises that he loves us and that we are precious to him: We are engraved on the palms of his hands (see Isaiah 49:16).

All of these benefits and more . . . because we have a relationship with God!

How to Be Sure You're a Christian

No couple can build a lasting marriage if one partner is unsure of the love of the other. What if a spouse isn't even sure if the other person accepts him or her completely and doubts the other's commitment for life? A marriage with that degree of uncertainty is unstable and unhealthy. The same is true in our relationship with God. People who aren't sure of their salvation can never fully experience the blessing of their union with Christ. On the other hand, there are people who assume they will go to heaven while failing to ask what might still stand in the way. These people may live with false hope and may possibly face eternal destruction.

In this study, we will examine some of the most common misconceptions about salvation. The purpose of this session is to help you be assured of your salvation and eternal destiny.

STUDY

When it comes to assurance of their salvation, people fall into three categories:

- Those who live with confidence that they have salvation

- Those who at times doubt their salvation

- Those who hope they are forgiven but lack assurance

Which category best describes you?

False Assurances of Salvation

Examine the following assumptions.

I'm assured of salvation because:

"I believe there is a God."

"I'm basically a good person."

"I attend church and pray often."

"I was baptized or confirmed."

"I once prayed a prayer and asked God into my heart."

1   "I believe there is a God."

How can a person believe in God and yet not have salvation?

2   "I'm basically a good person."

Why is trusting in our own goodness a false basis for being included in God's kingdom?

3   "I attend church and pray often."

Why doesn't being religious give enough assurance of salvation?

4 "I was baptized or confirmed."

Why could a person have been baptized yet not have assurance of salvation?

5 "I once prayed a prayer and asked God into my heart."

How could a person invite God into his or her heart and still not have a relationship with God?

Genuine Assurance of Salvation

Read John 1:12.

According to this verse, what do we do?

According to this verse, what does God do?

Read John 5:24.

According to this verse, what do we do?

According to this verse, what does God do?

Three Tests for Those Who Want to Be Sure

1   The repentance test

What does it mean for a person to repent? (Acts 3:19)

2   The presence test

What does the Holy Spirit do for a believer? (Romans 8:15-16)

3   The evidence test

What will be true of someone who has an authentic relationship with Christ? (1 John 2:3-6)

Conclusion

Read 1 John 5:11-13.   What does the phrase "that you may know" mean for us?

YOUR WALK WITH GOD

Central to the values behind the *Walking With God Series* is the belief that "homework" should not compete with a believer's regular appointments with God. Therefore, in this curriculum, a person's walk with God *is* the homework. Considering the pace of modern life, we thought it impractical for the average person to complete lengthy assignments *and* have quiet times. This material was designed to help you with the minimum requirements we considered necessary to maintain a vital connection with God.

To help you follow the regular assignments in this series, we have prepared the *Walking With God Journal.* In addition to providing pages for writing out the assignments, the journal contains practical advice on Bible study, prayer, and memorization. You'll also find suggestions for keeping quiet times fresh and creative tips on how to apply Bible knowledge to your life.

Bible

Make three appointments with God. Read 1 John chapters 1–2 and list as many ways as possible for a person to know that he or she is a Christian. Also read "What Is God Like?"

Prayer

Pray over any concerns that come to mind. Also, identify something for which you can be thankful.

Scripture Memory

I write these things to you who believe in the name of the Son of God so that you may know that you have eternal life.   1 John 5:13

Next time we will begin the first of two lessons on personal Bible study. If you want to prepare for the study, think about different ways that you can get teachings of the Bible into your life. Then consider why the Bible is important and what it does for us.

ON YOUR OWN

What Is God Like?

Most people think they know the answer to that question. It wouldn't even occur to them that they might not have an accurate picture of God. "Everybody knows what God is like! He's, uh, well he's . . ." What follows is a mishmash of ideas heard from parents and teachers over the years, never critically examined but firmly believed. At an even deeper level, what people *feel* toward God flows out of their life experiences—and is equally subjective and untested.

> "My grandma talked about God, and she was very nice to me—I guess I see God like her."

> "I grew up in a very strict home with lots of rules—pretty much like God treats me now."

> "Most ministers say God loves me—I guess he's like that."

> "Most ministers say God is really mad at me—I guess he's like that."

Let's begin with this assumption: some of our perspectives of God are wrong. We've seen too much, been hurt too much, been confused too much to assert we've got an accurate picture of God in every area. Somehow we got some misinformation—every one of us. So we'll either have to take deliberate steps to reeducate ourselves about what he's like, or our view of him will continue out of focus . . . and will probably get worse with time.

Where do we begin to get an accurate picture? A good place to start is with what God has done—by seeing his acts, we can get a picture of the one responsible. Just as art tells us something about the artist, or a person's work

24

tells us about his or her abilities and interests, what God has created tells us about what he, the Creator, is like. As we look at creation—nature, the world, the stars and galaxies—one undeniable conclusion emerges: the one responsible for all this must be powerful beyond comparison. From the tiniest single-cell amoeba to entire distant galaxies racing at near the speed of light, from an intricately complex snowflake to a sunset that sends amber blasts of color across the expansive sky, God's handiwork is so evident that you actively have to suppress what you see and feel in order to ignore him.

Yet the Bible tells us that's exactly what we do (Romans 1:18-20). That inner sense of his majesty—clearly evident in the cosmos—is squelched. We hear the Voice . . . and ignore it. And so while we all carry around some sense of his grandeur, we've modified and molded our image of him until the gap between who we perceive him to be and who he really is becomes uncrossable. Sin—our deliberate attempts to expel him from the throne of the universe as well as our passive indifference to his rule—not only messes up our lives, it messes up our view of God.

But our condition is not hopeless. God doesn't just *do*—he *speaks*. He talks to us. He sends messages. He tells us the truth through prophets and leaders. The Bible is the written record of his love. We learn from this book things we couldn't know otherwise.

For one thing, we learn that the sense of awe we get from his creation needs to be cultivated and expanded. Every notion we have of his power is true and then some. But we learn also that his power is restrained. He isn't an angry father about to blow his cool. He's a loving Father desiring to be close. In the earliest parts of the Bible we see God calling out a single man, Abraham, for a special purpose: to make a nation that would represent him to the world. That group of people was intended to be a tangible picture of his love, power, justice, and holiness. They'd be different from the rest of the world—because he is different. They'd be holy—because he is holy. They'd show compassion—because he is compassionate. They'd avoid sin—because he has no sin. They'd be blessed—because it's his nature to bless. Next to the picture of God painted in creation would be this picture painted through a unique group of people. He would talk to them and talk *through* them.

But God didn't just *do* and didn't just *speak*. He *became*. His work ordered the nothingness and made it a world for all to see. His word came to the prophets and made a book for all to read. The pinnacle of his communication was his Word coming to dwell among us in Jesus for all to receive. We *see* his handiwork; we *read* his book; we *meet* his Son. Jesus is the ultimate picture of God—the work and Word of God incarnate. What he does, God does. What he loves, God loves. What he hates, God hates. What he says, God says. How he acts, God acts. Look no further for clarification of what God is like: the only begotten Son has fully explained him (John 1:18). He showed God's awesome power by stilling the storm, healing the sick, and raising the dead—creation was subject to him. He showed God's desire to speak to us by unsurpassed teaching—truth was fully represented by him. And he lived out God's compassion without compromising his righteousness—God's nature was completely embodied in him. Nowhere was this more forcefully demonstrated than through his death on our behalf. By hating sin, God shows justice. By forgiving sin, he shows mercy. But by *being the payment* for that sin himself, he shows matchless, marvelous, magnificent grace.

This, then, is what God is like. Theologians have come up with words that summarize these qualities, or "attributes," as they're known. Once we get past the somewhat formal feel of these terms, they can be useful tools to encapsulate what we know about God. Here's a list of the main attributes.

What God Is—Ways We Can't Be Like Him

Omnipresent: God is always near; no place is farther from him than any other place; he is not limited to any spatial dimensions.

Omnipotent: God can do anything that doesn't violate his nature; he's all-powerful; nothing is impossible for him; his power is unlimited and unrestricted except by his own choice.

Omniscient: God knows everything; nothing is hidden; nothing goes unnoticed; no situation is beyond his ability to grasp; all mysteries are clear to him; no one can tell him something he doesn't already know.

Sovereign: God is the ultimate ruler of the universe; no one is greater in authority or power than he; no sin or disobedience can thwart the purposes he desires to bring to pass.

Eternal: God has always been; he will always be; he had no beginning; he'll have no end; he is the creator of time; he is not subject to time but rules over it.

Immutable: God doesn't change; he isn't getting better; his beauty can't be diminished; he doesn't grow or increase; he's perfect the way he is, and we can rest assured he will continue that way.

Infinite: God is unlimited; whatever he is, he is to an infinite degree; you can't measure any part of him or his attributes; he is inexhaustible in every aspect of his being.

Who God Is—Ways We Should Imitate Him

Holy: God is pure; he's without fault; he can't be compared to anyone or anything because he's so different from all we've known or experienced.

Wise: God uses his knowledge skillfully; he makes sense; he is no fool; his counsel can be trusted.

Good: God has no evil and can do no evil; he works for the benefit of his creatures; he can be trusted with our well-being.

Just: God is fair; he doesn't tolerate unrighteousness; he will make sure every wrong will be made right; he is impartial.

Loving: Sacrifice is in God's very nature; he cares; he gives; he serves; he works to bring about what we need; he's compassionate; he's sensitive; he chooses to let us matter to him.

We can come up with many other words that describe him as well: merciful, kind, pure, righteous, patient, faithful, trustworthy, generous, awesome, majestic, etc. These qualities will all be, to some degree, aspects of the main attributes we've listed. The more you get to know the Bible, the more you'll discover the manifold descriptions of his nature. Look for new ways of describing him. Worship him for the many and varied facets of his being. Learn who he really is, so you can gradually replace the shadows in your mind with the substance of his true nature.

What is God like? Maybe this song says it best: "Jesus loves me this I know, for the Bible tells me so . . ."

God's Word to You

Think back to a time when you received a letter from a close friend or a special someone who was away on summer vacation or for the school year. How did you feel when you received the envelope? How long did you wait to read the letter inside?

It is puzzling, then, to consider that many Christians are interested in knowing what God is saying to them yet neglect to read the letters and messages God has prepared for them. The Bible is God's love letter to all those who trust in Christ. It makes sense, then, that we should learn all we can about God's Word, for it is his primary means of speaking to us. The purpose of this meeting is to help you understand the value of personal Bible study.

STUDY

Five Ways We Grasp God's Word

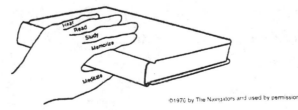

©1970 by The Navigators and used by permission

1 Hear (Romans 10:17)

What are some ways to hear God's Word?

2 Read (Revelation 1:3)

In what forms can you read God's Word?

3 Study (Acts 17:11)

What are some ways to study God's Word?

4 Memorize (Psalm 119:11)

What might be the benefits of memorizing God's Word?

5 Meditate (Psalm 1:2-3)

What does it mean to meditate on God's Word?

What Will God's Word Do for Me?

1 It will help me grow spiritually. (1 Peter 2:2)

What parallels can you see between an infant and its food and a Christian and the Bible?

2 It will help me be honest with myself. (Hebrews 4:12)

How does it feel to be "penetrated" by God's truth?

3 It equips me for good work. (2 Timothy 3:16-17)

Who is the author of the Bible?

What are the Scriptures good for in the life of the Christian?

4 It renews my mind. (Romans 12:2)

In what ways do you think God's Word could renew your mind?

5 It helps me be successful in life. (Joshua 1:8)

What is your view of success?

Additional Benefits

6 It puts truth at my fingertips. (2 Timothy 2:15)

What are some specific parallels between a workman and his tools and the Christian and his Bible?

7 It protects us from attack. (Ephesians 6:17)

How does the way a soldier uses a sword compare with how a Christian can use the Word?

8 It influences others. (Deuteronomy 6:6-7)

How does the Bible help you to have a spiritual influence on your family or others?

BOTTOM LINE

YOUR WALK WITH GOD

Bible

Read 1 John 3 the first day, 1 John 4 the second day, and 1 John 5 the third day. Make a list of all the truths in these chapters that have to do with love (love to others, love to God, love from God, and so on).

Prayer

Pray for another person this week.

Scripture Memory

All Scripture is God-breathed and is useful for teaching, rebuking, correcting and training in righteousness, so that the man of God may be thoroughly equipped for every good work. 2 Timothy 3:16-17

Next time we will take a closer look at the difference between *reading* the Bible and *studying* the Bible. If you want to prepare, think back to a time when you had to study a book for a test. In what ways was that experience different from simply reading the material for pleasure?

God's Word in You

The difference between Bible reading and Bible study is often a pencil. When we write things down, we achieve greater clarity and deeper understanding, making lessons learned easier to integrate into life. In the same way that we might find a rare nugget of gold lying on the ground, we can happen upon some valuable truths by simply browsing through the pages of Scripture. But to find a richer vein of gold, we have to go beneath the surface—and this discovery requires study.

While some may enjoy study for its own sake, the purpose of this lesson is to show how Bible study allows us to uncover truths that can transform our character. This study will help you learn how to use an inductive method to study the Bible.

STUDY

Four Approaches to Personal Bible Study

1   The Sitters

These people do not do personal Bible study at all. They would rather "sit at the feet" of someone who will explain the Bible to them.

What are the sitters missing by not studying the Bible themselves?

2   The Skimmers

These people go beyond the sitters and actually read God's Word themselves. They may also regularly read some kind of daily devotional book.

What do the skimmers miss by not going deeper into the Word?

3   The Scholars

This group of people, though small in number, is very much at home when studying the Bible in a scholarly manner, assisted by commentaries, Bible dictionaries, and other reference tools.

Why might the "scholars" find that their methods do not necessarily produce spiritual growth?

4   The Students

These people are like the person Paul describes in 2 Timothy 2:15. This is the category your group members should want to be in.

Read 2 Timothy 2:15.   What qualities does the "workman" Paul describes possess?

A Five-Step Inductive Bible Study Method

Step 1: Background

What kind of questions might you ask to learn more about the background of any book or passage that you are studying?

Step 2: Read

Why is it a good idea to read a whole book of the Bible completely through before analyzing its parts?

Step 3: Observe

How do you determine what a passage of Scripture is saying?

Step 4: Apply

How do you apply what you learn to your daily life?

Is there a promise to claim?

Is there a command to obey?

Is there sin to confess?

Is there an example to follow?

Is there a behavior to change?

Is there an encouragement to receive?

Is there an insight to gain?

Is there an issue to pray about?

Is there a reason to worship God?

Step 5: Memorize

Why is memorization important for personal Bible study?

BROAM

Background, Read, Observe, Apply, Memorize

Practice: Observe and Apply

Turn to James 1:2-4 to see how this inductive method works on an actual portion of Scripture. This abbreviated study will emphasize two of the five steps—*observation* and *application*—because you will spend most of your time doing these steps during your appointments with God.

Observation: "What does it say?"	Application: "What should I do?"

Bible

Study James 1 on three different occasions and list observations and applications. You may either study the whole chapter three times (perhaps using a different version each time) or read one-third of the chapter each time so the assignment is completed by the next study. Make one personal application for each day of study. Attempt to make your applications as specific as possible.

Prayer

In addition to your own personal concerns, pray this week for a particular ministry within your church.

Scripture Memory

Review verses you have learned so far: Revelation 3:20; 1 John 5:13; 2 Timothy 3:16-17.

In the next study we will learn more about the importance of memorizing Scripture. To prepare, try to recall the last time you had to memorize something for an important event. What helped you remember the information most effectively?

5

Taking God's Word to Heart

Imagine that you are a carpenter starting the first day at a new work site. As you begin your first task, you remember that all your tools are at home in your basement! You drive back home, get your hammer, and return to work. The same happens when you need a saw. Everyone else on the job is frustrated by the slowdown of having to wait for you. This pattern continues the rest of the day—every time you need a tool, you have to go home and get it. The situation gets worse later in the day when you cut your hand badly. The ambulance arrives within minutes, but the paramedics have to return to the hospital to get *their* equipment. They promise to get back to you as soon as they can.

A bad dream, right? This whole scene seems intolerable because of one obvious oversight: those who need their tools don't have them when and where they need them.

Yet many Christians approach their daily activities with a similar unpreparedness. They often neglect to carry with them the truths and promises of God's Word. Because it isn't always practical to flip to the Bible when faced with a difficult situation, Christians need more than just familiarity with the Scriptures—they need knowledge of what God says *on the spot and at the moment.* And one of the best ways to have his Word readily accessible is through memorization. This study will help you understand the importance and benefits of memorizing Scripture.

Read Luke 4:1-13.   What do you observe about Jesus' responses to the devil?

In what kinds of situations might having passages of Scripture committed to memory be helpful to you?

Great Reasons to Memorize Scripture

In what way can memorizing Scripture . . .

1   *Purify your thoughts? (Philippians 4:8)*

2   *Increase your effectiveness in prayer? (John 15:7)*

3   *Be useful in witnessing? (Acts 8:35-36)*

4   *Help you meditate? (see Psalm 119:97)*

5   *Enrich your Bible study? (2 Timothy 3:16)*

6   *Enhance your counseling or teaching? (Proverbs 15:23)*

7   *Provide guidance for decisions? (Psalm 119:24)*

8   *Provide encouragement when you're feeling down? (Romans 15:4)*

9   *Strengthen you when tempted? (Psalm 37:31)*

10 *Increase your faith? (Romans 10:17)*

Helps for Memorization

What do you see as the value of each of these steps?

1 **Focus on the benefit**

2 **Know the meaning**

3 **Use your imagination**

4 **Don't forget to review**

5 **Involve others**

Meditation and Memorization

What does it mean to meditate on God's Word?

Read Psalm 119:97.   When is the best time of the day for meditation?

Note: For additional insights on memorizing Scripture, see Bob Siefert, "You Can Memorize Scripture," in *Discipleship Journal* (Issue 9, 1982), p. 36, and Francis Cosgrove, *The Essentials of Discipleship* (Colorado Springs: NavPress, 1980).

BOTTOM LINE

Bible

Read James 2 in each of your three appointments with God this week. List observations and at least one application for each time of Bible study.

Prayer

Pray that God will help you memorize his Word and internalize it so that you are better able to do what the Bible says (James 1:22).

Scripture Memory

I have hidden your word in my heart that I might not sin against you.   Psalm 119:11

In the next study we will begin to explore the topic of prayer. To prepare, think about a time that you prayed for something specific. What happened or didn't happen as a result of your prayer? What principles about prayer would you give to a new believer?

6

Ground Rules for Prayer

Would you prefer reading a book by candlelight or by a bright overhead light? If you're like most people, you would choose the overhead light. Although candlelight has a certain beauty about it, it's quite limited in the amount of light it can give. Besides, a gust of wind could blow it out or someone could easily extinguish it. To accomplish any amount of reading without severe eyestrain, we need the overhead light to illuminate the book's pages. And to get this light, we must use a switch.

In the spiritual realm, prayer is the switch that allows the power of the Holy Spirit to illuminate our lives. Many Christians live their lives guided only by their own natural light, their own wisdom and power. But by using the switch of prayer, the Holy Spirit intercedes and causes the Father's light to bathe our lives. Prayer is the difference—the power is there already. It just has to be "switched on." This study will help you understand how God answers prayer. We will explore four principles of prayer from the Bible and the four kinds of answers that God gives.

Four Principles of Prayer

1 The Holy Spirit helps us to know what and how to pray (Romans 8:26)

In what ways are we weak when it comes to prayer?

Describe a time when you were frustrated with not knowing how to pray.

2 The Holy Spirit intercedes on our behalf (Romans 8:26)

What do you think are some of the personal benefits of having the Holy Spirit pray for you?

3 God hears our hearts in prayer more than our words (Romans 8:27)

What comfort is there in knowing that God searches our hearts?

Read Matthew 6:5-8. What "errors" in prayer does Jesus mention?

4 Prayer is always answered (Romans 8:28-29)

In what ways might God be at work even when he doesn't give an immediate "yes" to our prayers?

Four Ways God Answers Prayer

1 No—Your request is wrong (Matthew 26:36-39)

What are some examples of prayer requests you know God would say "no" to?

2 Slow—Your timing is wrong (John 11:1-6)

What are some examples of prayer requests that God might say "slow" to?

3 Grow—Your spiritual condition is wrong (James 4:2-3)

In what ways might God ask you to grow before he gives you a "yes" to a prayer?

4 Go—Your request, timing, and spiritual condition are OK (Acts 12:5-17)

What are some of your prayers that God has answered with a "yes"?

What will it take for you to become a person who prays more?

Bible

Keep three appointments with God, studying James 3:1-18.   Note observations and applications. Also, reread the Scripture passages from the section "Four Ways God Answers Prayer."

Prayer

Pray about those areas in your life where you need God's wisdom and strength.

Scripture Memory

Do not be anxious about anything, but in everything, by prayer and petition, with thanksgiving, present your requests to God. And the peace of God, which transcends all understanding, will guard your hearts and your minds in Christ Jesus.
Philippians 4:6-7

We will learn more about prayer in the next study. Thinking through the following questions will help you prepare for the session. Did you ever have a friend or family member who seemed to be always asking you for things? What was missing from that relationship? What do you like most about your current prayer life? What do you like least?

7

Let's Pray

When you took industrial arts or home economics in junior high or middle school, the assignment you did for the grade was also something you could take home and use. Perhaps you made a book rack or a blouse or even something good to eat. Learning about prayer is similar. In this study you will not only learn an effective way of praying, but you will also practice praying—and God will give you his answers "to take home with you"!

This study will show you a simple method for a more balanced prayer life. The first part will present the A.C.T.S. outline to help you structure your prayers. This will allow you to overcome the natural tendency to pray only about things you want. The second part will allow everyone to practice the A.C.T.S. pattern for prayer.

STUDY

What are some principles of prayer that you learned in the previous study? (Romans 8:26-29)

A.C.T.S.: A Way to Pray

Adoration (Psalm 100:1-5)

How do you express adoration?

What benefits come to us from praising God?

Confession (1 John 1:9)

Why is it difficult to confess our sin to God?

What does God promise he will do when we confess our sin?

Thanksgiving (Luke 17:11-19)

What excuses keep you from giving thanks to God?

Supplication (Philippians 4:6-7)

What are some specific examples of requests we can bring to God in prayer?

If God knows all of our needs, why should we specify them through prayer?

What role does faith play in supplication?

Prayer Time

Adoration

Father, I want to praise you for being _____.

Confession

What are some examples of sinful behavior, thoughts, or attitudes Christians should confess?

Thanksgiving

Thank you, Lord, for giving me _____.

Supplication

What one or two major concerns are on your mind today?

BOTTOM LINE

Bible

Study James 4:1-17, noting observations and applications.

Prayer

Practice each of the four aspects of prayer—one each day.

Day One: Praise God using Psalm 23.

Day Two: Identify the main areas of temptation you struggle with. Confess any sin in these areas and pray for strength.

Day Three: Recall several spiritual, physical, and relational blessings. Thank God for each one.

Day Four: Pray for any major concerns in your life and in the lives of others who are close to you.

Scripture Memory

Be joyful always; pray continually; give thanks in all circumstances, for this is God's will for you in Christ Jesus. 1 Thessalonians 5:16-18

In the next study we will examine how regular quiet times can enhance your walk with God. To prepare for the session, ask yourself the following questions: What is one area of your walk with God with which you could use some help? What would be the consequences if the Holy Spirit were not in your life at all?

Getting Together with God

After driving through miles of gridlock to arrive early to work, a busy executive closes his office door to enjoy a few moments of quiet before the phones begin ringing. . . . A frazzled mother puts her noisy children to bed and plops down on the couch in the stillness of the evening to talk at last with her husband. . . . A weary student takes a break from a frantic exam schedule to take an unhurried walk around campus.

What do all these people have in common? They need times of quiet and calm to relax, think about the day, and to build relationships with friends and family. In a similar way, we also need times of quiet and prayerful reflection with the Lord and his Word to build our relationship with him.

How do we do that? Scheduling regular quiet times is a good way to start. This study will give you some practical advice for establishing regular times for personal devotions.

What Is a Quiet Time?

How would you describe a good quiet time?

What do you do during your times alone with God?

Making the Time

Why is it difficult for us to find time for personal devotions?

Here are some ways to find time in a crowded schedule:

- Listen to a cassette tape of worshipful music as you drive, work around the house, or get ready for the day.
- Take a walk or ride in the car to a forest preserve, the country, or other place of natural beauty.
- Sing worshipful songs to the Lord.
- Occasionally vary your quiet time routine so that you don't get stuck in a rut.

What could you do to make your times alone with God more meaningful?

Studying the Bible

What hinders you from getting more out of personal Bible study?

Here are some ways to vary your study of the Scripture:

- Use a concordance to study a specific topic, character trait, or Bible character.
- Use the cross references in the margin of your Bible to study a topic.
- Meditate on a passage by creating vivid mental pictures of the story or event.
- Rewrite the passage, using contemporary wording or your own circumstances as the setting.
- Mark interesting phrases that stand out to you.
- Write down questions as you read.
- Write a short title to describe the passage you are reading.
- Listen to the Bible on tape.

What are some other creative ways of making your Bible study more meaningful?

Praying

What prevents you from praying consistently?

Here are some other variations you can use to keep your prayer life fresh:

- Write out your prayers.
- Keep a prayer journal to record your prayers and answers.
- Vary the A.C.T.S. pattern so that you spend one day in adoration, another in confession, and so on.

- Put away your prayer list and simply talk to God.
- Vary your position, posture, or location when you pray.

What other ideas do you have to make your prayer time more effective?

Action Plan

What is the best time of day for you to have your quiet time?

What is the best place for you to have your quiet time?

What are the most likely distractions or interruptions you will face?

What can you do to prevent these distractions or interruptions?

BOTTOM LINE

Bible

Study James 5:1-20, noting observations and applications.

Prayer

Pray that you may become the kind of person who does what the Bible says (James 1:22).

Scripture Memory

Review the verses from the previous three lessons: Psalm 119:11; Philippians 4:6-7; 1 Thessalonians 5:16-18.

Next time we will begin the first of four studies on the Holy Spirit. To prepare, recall how you first learned about the Holy Spirit.

The Role of the Holy Spirit

Think for a moment about the way wind affects our lives. It is often a gentle current that refreshes us on a hot day. It is the steady breeze that keeps a child's kite aloft and guides a sailboat to its destination. Then, too, the wind can be a tremendous force of nature, whipping snow into gigantic snow drifts, knocking down power lines, and grounding airplanes. We must learn to respect its power or we may find ourselves in danger.

Jesus compared the Holy Spirit to wind (see John 3:8). Like the wind, the Spirit can assist us in our efforts to please God, and he also intervenes to discourage us from sinful activity. His power must not be resisted, however, because to do so affronts God and cuts us off from our source. Cooperation with the Holy Spirit is essential for any Christian's walk with God. Who is the Holy Spirit and what does he do? This study will help you understand the person and work of the Holy Spirit.

Who Is the Holy Spirit?

Read John 14:16-26.

What titles does Jesus use to describe the Holy Spirit? (John 14:16-17)

Who sent the Holy Spirit? (John 14:26)

Why can't the world accept the Spirit? (John 14:17)

What Is the Role of the Holy Spirit?

In what way does the Holy Spirit convict us? (John 16:7-11)

How does the Holy Spirit guide us? (John 16:12-15)

In what way does the Holy Spirit teach us? (John 14:26)

How does the Holy Spirit help to save us? (Titus 3:5)

What does it mean when we say the Holy Spirit reassures us? (Romans 8:15-16)

In what way is the Spirit like a deposit? (Ephesians 1:13-14)

For what does the Holy Spirit empower us? (Acts 1:8)

How does the Holy Spirit help us when we pray? (Romans 8:26)

What role of the Spirit impressed you in this study?

How would you summarize the ministry of the Holy Spirit to a new Christian?

BOTTOM LINE

Bible

Study Philippians 1:1-30 three times this week. Make one observation about this passage each day. Make a specific application for each observation.

Prayer

Day One: List temptations you face and write down what you could do to better resist them.

Day Two: List some physical or material blessings (ones you normally don't think of).

Day Three: Pray about a major concern in your life.

Scripture Memory

Do not get drunk on wine, which leads to debauchery. Instead, be filled with the Spirit. Ephesians 5:18

In the next study we will discover what it means to be filled with the Holy Spirit. To prepare, ask yourself: What are some things that can fill or dominate a person's life? Also, if the Holy Spirit is in our lives as Christians, why don't our lives reflect Jesus Christ more clearly?

10

Being Filled with the Holy Spirit

Imagine filling two glasses with equal amounts of water. Into one glass you drop a seltzer tablet that is wrapped in a plastic bag. You notice that nothing happens—the plastic has prevented the tablet from dissolving in the water. Now you drop an unwrapped tablet into the other glass. The tablet fizzes exuberantly and fills the glass with hundreds of small bubbles.

This simple experiment illustrates how we should allow the Holy Spirit to work in our lives. When we do not face our sin and hinder his work, our disobedience acts like the plastic bag around the seltzer and robs us of the Spirit's dynamic influence. But when we are receptive and obedient to God, the Holy Spirit releases his energy into every part of our life. This study will show you how the Holy Spirit can fill your life and what his work in you accomplishes.

How did we describe the role of the Holy Spirit in the last study?

What is the Holy Spirit's role in the process of our spiritual growth? (Philippians 1:6)

What is our role in the process of spiritual growth? (Ephesians 5:18)

What does it mean to say that Christians should be "filled" with the Holy Spirit?

What are some things being filled with the Spirit helps us to do? (Ephesians 5:19-21)

How does being filled with the Spirit influence our character? (Galatians 5:22-23)

Recall the illustration. What does the plastic bag around the seltzer tablet represent?

What would cause you to seal in or limit the power of the Spirit in your life?

How do we "unwrap" and turn loose the Holy Spirit's influence in us?

In what areas have you allowed the Holy Spirit to permeate your life?

BOTTOM LINE

YOUR WALK WITH GOD

Bible

Study Philippians 2:1-30, making at least three applications and observations.

Prayer

Day One: Adoration—meditate on Psalm 103:1-5 and express a prayer of adoration in your own words.

Day Two: Thanksgiving—thank God for relationships with specific people that have been a blessing to you and others.

Day Three: Concerns—pray for three of your own and three from other people (you may pray about the concerns shared at the beginning of this study).

Scripture Memory

I have been crucified with Christ and I no longer live, but Christ lives in me. The life I live in the body, I live by faith in the Son of God, who loved me and gave himself for me. Galatians 2:20

In the next study we will look at how believers can be filled with the Spirit. Consider these questions: Describe something that is now a habit for you that had to be learned over time. How did that behavior, practice, or discipline become second nature? As a Christian, what changes in your life have come easily? What changes have come with difficulty? What changes aren't coming at all?

How to Be Filled with the Holy Spirit

A brash young entrepreneur decides to start a business in a lucrative, high-tech field. Because he needs the help, he brings on board a top-flight consultant to function as his daily advisor. But instead of trusting in the consultant's wisdom, the entrepreneur decides to do things his way. He ignores directives about financial planning. He makes ill-advised decisions without his advisor's knowledge. He even keeps him out of important meetings. Predictably, the business fails within a short time.

Many Christians fail to realize that their relationship with the Lord shares many of the same problems. These people know about the wisdom of a daily quiet time and may even want the Spirit to direct their lives. But they insist on doing things their own way. It comes as no surprise that they stumble again and again. These setbacks are entirely preventable, however. This study will show you how you can live in the Spirit more fully each day.

What changes in your life will occur as a result of being filled with the Holy Spirit?

How Can I Be Filled with the Holy Spirit?

1 Surrender to Christ

What are Christians to put to death? (Colossians 3:1-5)

What does it mean for a Christian to become a living sacrifice? (Romans 12:1-2)

Read both Luke 18:22-23 and 19:5-8.   How would you compare the ways in which these two men faced the need to surrender to God?

Self-Directed Living

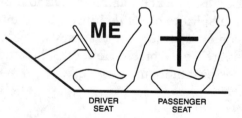

What problems will result from a self-directd life?

Spirit-Directed Living

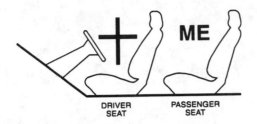

DRIVER
SEAT

PASSENGER
SEAT

What traits will a Spirit-directed life produce?

2 Obey Christ

Once you have surrendered (an inward change) the next step is to obey (an outward change).

What happens when Christians surrender but do not obey? (1 John 2:3-6)

List a few areas of your life that are important to you. What does it mean to obey Christ in each area?

3 Abide in Christ

To abide in Christ means to continue or remain in him. Why is abiding in Christ important? (John 15:1-11)

How can you tell when you are not abiding in Christ?

Conclusion

How can you live in the Spirit more fully each day?

BOTTOM LINE

YOUR WALK WITH GOD

Bible

Do a study of Philippians 3:1-21 at least three times, noting observations and applications.

Prayer

Look up the following passages that relate to obeying Christ. On each of four days, pray for the two areas listed that should be surrendered to Christ's control.

Day One: The future (Proverbs 3:5-6; James 4:13-17) and relationships (Matthew 5:21-26; Romans 12:9-21)

Day Two: Work (Colossians 3:22–4:1; Psalm 127:1-2) and leisure (Mark 6:31-32; Ephesians 5:15-16)

Day Three: Marriage (Matthew 19:4-6; 1 Peter 3:1-9) and children (Colossians 3:21; Psalm 127:3-5) or if you are single, another significant relationship

Day Four: Money (Psalm 112:5; 1 Corinthians 16:1-2) and possessions (Matthew 6:31-33; Luke 12:13-21)

Scripture Memory

Anyone, then, who knows the good he ought to do and doesn't do it, sins.   James 4:17

Next time we will discuss how we can grieve the Holy Spirit—ways in which we hinder his work. To prepare, think about the different ways a person can suppress or extinguish a fire. What parallels can you draw between those conditions and the ways a believer can put out the fire of the Holy Spirit?

Grieving the Holy Spirit

Imagine that you are sitting around a campfire on a cool autumn evening. The warmth of the flames makes you feel comfortable and content. You become lost in your thoughts when, without warning, a sudden shower pours down on your campsite. The leaping flames soon turn into flickers, then become smoldering ashes. Now you are wet and miserable, and the chill of the evening makes you long for the glow that you felt a few moments earlier.

In much the same way, we can quench the fire of the Holy Spirit with careless actions and sinful attitudes. Not only do we cause God anguish, but we become miserable ourselves. This study will help you understand what it means to grieve the Holy Spirit and how to get back in step with the Spirit when you do.

STUDY

Grieving the Holy Spirit

What are some ways to cause a friend or parent to grieve?

73

What does it mean to grieve the Holy Spirit? (Ephesians 4:29-31)

What does it mean to put out the Spirit's fire? (1 Thessalonians 5:19-22)

Ways We Grieve the Holy Spirit

1   Active disobedience (sins of commission)

What are some example of active disobedience? (Galatians 5:16-21)

Why does active disobedience grieve the Spirit?

2   Passive disobedience (sins of omission)

What is passive disobedience? (James 4:17)

What are some examples of knowing the right thing to do but not doing it?

3 Being ashamed of Christ

What consequences will a believer suffer for being ashamed of Christ ? (Mark 8:38)

In what situations do you find it difficult to stand up for Christ?

4 Lack of faith in Christ

Read Mark 9:17-23. Who lacked faith in this story?

How should we respond when we lack faith? (Mark 9:24)

Why does lack of faith grieve the Holy Spirit? (Hebrews 11:6)

In what way do you frequently grieve the Holy Spirit?

What should we do when we think we are grieving the Holy Spirit?

BOTTOM LINE

YOUR WALK WITH GOD

Bible

Study Philippians 4:1-23 three times, writing down your observations and applications.

Prayer

Day One: Adoration—read Psalm 103:15-22 and praise God for his love and righteousness.

Day Two: Confession—pray about anything mentioned in this study that you feel convicted about. Be specific.

Day Three: Supplication—pray for members of your family who have emotional, physical, or relational needs.

Scripture Memory

Review the memory verses from the previous three studies: Ephesians 5:18; Galatians 2:20; James 4:17.

Next time we will review the previous topics in this study. To prepare, look back through studies 1–12. Which topic was most memorable to you? In what ways have you seen progress in your Christian life?

Reviewing Friendship with God

This review culminates your study of *Friendship With God,* the first book in the *Walking With God Series*. Use this time to reflect on your small group experience so far. This is also a time to appreciate and be grateful for what God has accomplished in you. This study will help you assess what you've learned and how you've grown.

STUDY

Since we began, what have you found to be the most positive aspect of these studies?

Identify a fresh insight or an old truth that has come alive through this study.

What area of your personal spiritual growth needs improvement?

How has your understanding of the Bible changed since you began this study?

What is one change you've noticed in your prayer life as a result of this study?

How would you describe the importance of quiet time to someone who just became a Christian?

What is the significance of the Holy Spirit in the life of the believer?

Currently, what is the greatest obstacle to your walk with God?

Ten years from now, what you like your walk with God to be like?

I would like everyone to pray for _____.

YOUR WALK WITH GOD

Bible

Study three times Matthew 4:1-25 (in preparation for the first study in *The Incomparable Jesus.*)

Prayer

Day One: Adoration—pray in accordance with Psalm 91:1-2.

Day Two: Confession—what is something you've found difficult to do in recent days that you know you should do?

Day Three: Thanksgiving—thank God for the promises he has given us about the future.

Scripture Memory

Review the following verses: Revelation 3:20; 1 John 5:13; 2 Timothy 3:16–17; Psalm 119:11; Philippians 4:6–7; 1 Thessalonians 5:16–18; Ephesians 5:18; Galatians 2:20; James 4:17.

Self-Evaluation

Your group leader will be meeting with you to discuss your current spiritual condition and your hopes for growing in your faith. Please take some time to reflect honestly on where you stand right now within these four basic categories of Christian growth. Rate yourself in each category.

+ Doing well. I'm pleased with my progress so far.

✓ On the right track, but I see definite areas for improvement.

— This is a struggle. I need some help.

A Disciple Is One Who . . .

Walks with God

To what extent is my Bible study and prayer time adequate for helping me walk with God?

Rating:

Comments:

Lives the Word

To what extent is my mind filled with scriptural truths so that my actions and reactions show I am being transformed?

Rating:

Comments:

Contributes to the work

To what extent am I actively participating in the church with my time, talents, and treasures?

Rating:

Comments:

Impacts the world

To what extent am I impacting my world with a Christian witness and influence?

Rating:

Comments:

Other issues I would like to discuss with my small group leader:

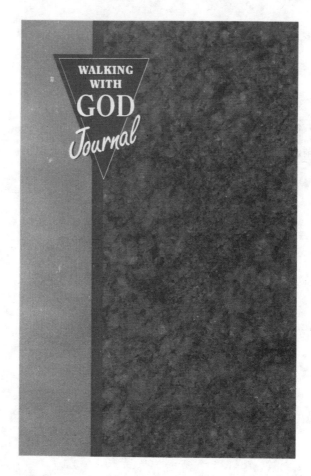

The *Walking With God Journal* is the perfect companion to the *Walking With God Series*. Use it to keep your notes during Bible study, record your prayers, or simply jot down your thoughts and insights. (0-310-91642-9)